1. An Introduction

Exponential resource management isn't just a fancy name. It's a really underestimated, under used marketing method that works incredibly well. So much so, this section is one of the main reasons we're only letting 500 copies of this go. I don't want my competition to be able to manage their customers correctly if it means I'm going to get them instead.

What we're looking at here are your five primary resources. The lifeblood of any online business. That's your affiliates, your list, your customers, long term customers and joint venture prospects. All of which we'll refer to from this point onwards as your resources, or your promotion power.

Each one of the big five have the power to make you sales, and thus big profits. However, imagine being able to take those five and manage them in such a way that you never have to carry out the expensive act of paying for new customers, a bigger, list, more affiliates or JV contacts ever again, but still having countless thousands of them flowing into your lap.

It sounds unthinkable, but with the right management of your resources, you're going to be seeing their usefulness double, multiply by three, four, sometimes even five. What does this mean or your profits? Well, have you ever worked it out in your head how much you'd make if you doubled a penny every day for a month or two? The principal here is the same, but instead of money, you're using your resources. The more you have, the faster they build each other. The true power of real exponential growth is at every marketers fingertips. They just have to know how to realize it's there and understand how to use it to their advantage..

2. The Goals Of This Section

• To demonstrate how to take your existing resources and cross them over in such a way that they begin to build themselves. The ultimate in marketing strategies allowing you to boost your promotion power exponentially, when others are having trouble even building a list that makes a single sale.

• To display a diagram to demonstrate this method helping you commit this to memory and act on your knowledge.

• To discuss each resource in depth and to define specific roles for each one, opening up the ability to cross your resources and to start the snowball effect rolling.

• To avoid the pitfalls that other marketers are making as we speak with their crossing of resources, if they've even discovered such a method in the first place.

• To inspire and to demonstrate ideas for the crossing of your resources, both enabling you to follow the examples we've laid out for you, and to come up with your own as your resources start to flood in when you launch your products.

3. Exponential Resource Management 1

Greetings, and welcome to the manual entitled exponential resource management and treating your customers right. As well as a selection of literal ways to get the most out of your customers without giving them the earth for free, we'll also be taking a little bit of a lateral detour here.

You see, when I say treating your customers right, I'm not just talking about how to keep your customers happy. Although this is important, what I'm going to show you is much *more* important, and much more beneficial to you, and it should alter the way you think about what you're doing and how you're doing it.

Resources. Your five main resources. Joint Ventures, Affiliates, Standard List, Standard Customers and Long Term Customers. That is exactly what this section is about. Not just being nice to people so they trust you more, we're going deeper than this to start with. We'll leave the easier stuff until afterwards.

3b. The Working Concept: An Overview.

The whole idea of this section is based around kind of a cross promotion strategy, which is nothing new products wise, but when we look at it in terms of the five main resources you've been gathering it becomes a different matter entirely. What we're planning to do here is take the whopping promotion power of the big five, tie them together and double what they're doing for you without bringing in anyone new. We're simply referring each type of member to different sections.

Now, you may have seen this circle of five before when talking in terms of website promotion, using the site itself as a base to launch each resource onto the next stage in the ladder where possible, whilst at the same time bringing in new blood. This time around, we're taking that circle, and moving people around so that they can reside in multiple places, which in turn, can double, or even triple your promotion power simply because one person becomes two, three and up to five different resources on their own. Powerful stuff. For quick reference, here's that basic resource circle that we're talking about. We'll be adding to this in a moment.

Now, this is going to become a big part of the circle, because it's going to add to it internally, as we're moving people around here without bringing in new people, increasing the productivity of the people we already have, so please do take a careful look at it right now, or the rest of this section won't make any sense. The main thing I want you to keep in mind is the above diagram, as that will form the basis of your whole web based marketing outlook. It will however be added to at the end of this manual, so that you have five large diagrams at the end of the course to base your marketing off of.

What we're going to do now is go through each resource, and look at the most effective ways to cross them over to another resource, whether it's worth doing, why you should or shouldn't do particular things with each section, and most importantly, which ones are going to make you the most cash.

Even if you don't have all of these resources at your disposal yet, don't worry. The aim here is to show you what's going to go on when your promotions do go out and be prepared. Let me assure you, the speed that the five main resources come in may turn around and surprise you, It's going to come in very handy, very soon.

3c. What to do with your list.

So first up, lets start with your list. Think first about what your list is. It's your first contact, and it contains pretty much everyone that's passed through the system you've set up, from the freebie hunters, to the people that didn't know what they signed up for, those who had friends that signed them up for a joke, and of course those who are going to progress through the circle and make you a whole load of cash in several different ways. It's the most numerous of all the five resources, and is also in this instance of the lowest quality compared to the other four, however is essential if you want to fill the higher ranks.

3d. An Important Tip.

Keep in mind that it's not always possible or even in your best interests to subject a particular resource to this type of cross promotion. This is especially true for your more valuable money-makers. The reason being is that they can be lost, just like any other resource, but when you take the regular customers who have spent many thousands of dollars on your products in small numbers, compared to a large list that have yet to spend, it's much more devastating to lose one or two percent of your big spenders than it is to lose one or two percent of your freebie seekers.

3e. What To Do With Your List Continued.

So, getting started here, what do we want to turn your list into? Well, everything really. Your lists are there for one thing, and one thing only, and that's to act as your own media outlet, and increase your other four resources. (something that many business miss). Turning your list into customers and long- term customers is quite straight forward. You'll be sending them announcements relating to your new products and services. It's as they should be used, and most often are.

Two more extremely profitable things that your list can do that people rarely ever seem to catch hold of (even more profitable than making direct sales) is build your affiliate base and on top of that build your joint venture base. First up the affiliate building. Remember we talked previously about promotion to build resources instead of make the profits? Well this works in exactly the same way. The reason we don't see it too often, aside from the people that have been told about it, or sussed it out already, is who in their right mind would promote, and in fact spend the two most important things (their money and their time) on promotion when they're not going to make any cash out of it directly.

The sooner that you, as an business-person, online or offline can see how important it is to look beyond immediate profits from ad campaigns, the sooner you will start to make some real money. I guess it's overlooked by so many simply because in today's age of the internet, everyone wants something right now, they don't want to wait. The longer it takes to carry out, the more they overlook it as something that won't be an immediate fix for their situation.

3f. Building Your Affiliates From Your List.

One thing I do want to say to you now is, if you have sixty five, seventy, eighty percent, or even more to give away through your products' commissions, don't be afraid to tell people about it. Not so long ago in fact, maybe two or three years prior to writing this report, there was a spate of big affiliate commission sites popping up that offered anywhere from 80-100% commissions that did incredibly well on the resource building side of things simply on the basis of promoting their high commissions more than the product itself.

So whatever you do, don't think that gaining affiliates is all about that little button at the top of your sites with 80% for affiliates written in big letters. Hey, we spend money to promote free products to build our lists all the time, why can't we do the same for our affiliates? Well we can, and to be honest, one good affiliate is more valuable than a hundred subscribers, even a thousand subscribers in my eyes, for the simple reason that they may have an audience of tens or even hundreds of thousands on their lists that they're willing to give you access to. Imagine the resources that would land in your lap, and the power you'll have for future promotion when a few ads like that start to go out. So the rule here is just this. If you're following the charts we've put up for you, this guide or a modified version of it, built around your own needs, and your commissions are higher than the average fifty percent, go ahead and make sure people know about it through your promotion. Make it a prime concern of yours and you won't be disappointed.

3g. Turing Your List Into Joint Ventures.

Now as far as turning your list into joint ventures goes, this is a pretty easy but also open ended and rather variable in results until you actually see what these people are capable of further down the line. Similar to previously, when we talked about gaining feedback from your list you can in the same way, gain joint ventures from your list, again, as in the above example with the affiliates, this is often far more widely used, and for good reason.

I urge you once again, not to relegate your joint venture prospects to those who visit your website, and the individuals you pick out through the top performing affiliates, but to actively seek them through your list. The reason we're doing this is simply because there's a good chance someone will be out there that won't progress down your line of resources otherwise. If they're experienced, have a big list of their own, or the ability to get in touch with your target market, you're going to miss out if you're not telling them that you want their services.

For example, an experienced marketer that subscribes to a selection of lists to keep up with what's going on around them, happens to subscribe to your list where you're selling an info product such as this. He or she won't buy your how to product, because they've got their system set up already and it just so happens, that they only promote their own stuff to their own lists, unless it's a joint venture (this is very common among the big guys by the way), they won't buy your big product for the same reason, and they won't be joining your affiliate program for the above reason. He or she is a heavy hitter with a big list, but you're missing out. These are the people you're aiming to cater for here. It's not good if you're leaving massive holes like this, because you're missing out on some massive profit potential. In fact, as we speak the majority of marketers out there are very obviously leaving these types of holes.

The problem with joint venturing through a list at this stage is it becomes kind of a lottery if you're not careful. You can't just send out a mailing asking for anyone with a list over ten thousand people to contact you for higher commissions, because then everyone else feels cheated and you may alienate some potential affiliates. In general terms joint ventures should be a private thing, the deal will also vary from person to person, depending on your product, their list size, what they want in return and what you can grant in return. The best way to go about this is to keep it that way.

Don't do a mass mailing just requesting joint ventures for the reasons above, we can't do that for this particular resource.

What I'd suggest you do instead, which you should be doing with your list anyway, is carry on as your normally do, sending out your un-intrusive surveys to help with your research and find out as much info as you can about the people on your list, for something in return. For example a short valuable report that you've written on your area of expertise. In exchange you're getting vital info that not only allows you to tailor your ads to your list providing a better response rate, but at the same time you're building up a picture of who the good joint venture prospects are. Once you've done that, you can go through the results you've collected, and pick the top performers, the knowledgeable, and the people with the most resources, and contact them individually.

3h What To Do With Your List Summarized.

So you see, your list is your first contact that you have with your customers and the potential is there to turn them into the other four resources further up the food chain if done as above. If it's related to your business, and other people should be seeing, reading, using, buying or promoting it, your list should know about it at least once, in it's unspecialized, most basic and standard form. Leave them in the dark, and you're missing out on potentially thousands, tens of thousands in profit, or more.

3i. What To Do With Your Customers.

Moving on from your list, and your most general and untargeted form of targeted marketing, lets take a look at the first specialized section here, your customers. The people that have either only bought low priced introductory products from you before, or have only purchased from you once.

What you'll start to see is as we get more specialized and move up the food chain in terms of profitability, things start to get easier to figure out what to do and when to do it when crossing your resources over. It's also important to note, that with paying customers, and them being lower in numbers than your list, it's easier to make a mistake and lose profit potential rather quickly if you're not careful about where you're setting foot.

When thinking about what to do with what resource, remember to always think in terms of where these people are going next in the standard form when setting orders in the way of importance. For example, with our short-term customers, in the standard flow of things, they'll be turning into your big buyers. The people that buy the most products from you at the highest price, so again, short term, they may not seem like much now, but in the future, this is where your big profits are going to be coming from, hence their major importance, and the general attitude is that you should give them something a little extra for their time. That's not because they're more demanding than your list, but because the profit potential is much higher for you, their numbers are much smaller, and the margin of error also is much smaller.

3j. Organizing Is The Key To Success.

Now before we even start, we're seeing a new problem emerge. The organizing and managing of five different resources that all overlap can become a complex, time consuming and confusing task, and that's not what we want. I can rightly see why many just take all their five resources and just bundle them into one list. I'd highly suggest you avoid doing this unless you're just promoting other peoples stuff or very rarely create your own products. If your business is, and will in the future remain all about the products you're creating and selling, keep them separate. If you carry this section out correctly, it won't mean a huge amount of extra work, aside from five short mailings per product promotion drive or launch instead of one.

3k. Back To Managing Your Customers.

The reason I mention the above is that when you get to this stage, the people out there that do things this way, and keep their resources separated, try to give them the earth. For example, if I told you how valuable these people are, and you wanted to turn them into affiliates, how do you do so?

The general answer would be to give them higher commissions. This however is not worth your trouble, because we're overlooking one serious flaw in that plan. Unless your product is geared to give higher commissions in the beginning to people who purchase it, these people aren't necessarily suited to affiliate material, and in my experience, it's best not to bombard them with affiliate signup pages and adverts about how much they can make unless that is a specific benefit of your product.

I'd suggest to you that the only way around this is not to do the above, because your main aim is not to make them promote for you, but to buy your higher priced products and move up the ladder. So the solution is treat them as such. When you're mailing them about a new product, include information about how much they can earn promoting for you. I highly recommend not deviating from the original plan and flow of the chart with these important people, especially when it comes to trying to turn them into affiliates. You'll gain plenty of them via the other resources, leave well alone trying to give them bonuses or bigger commissions at this stage, because otherwise you'll just end up with a big tangled ball of yarn and a headache. We'll get on to just how we make them valued in a moment.

But first, lets look at turning your customers into your list. To start with, you'll find that most of your customers are on your list anyway. Not much needs to be said about this subject for that very reason. Any customers that aren't on your standard list will still be receiving ads for your products, high cost products and low cost products as part of your introductory series each time you launch something new using the backend sales flow chart. What they won't be receiving are the mails that you use to try and separate your list into one of these categories for the same reasons as with the lack of affiliate mailings as explained in the previous point.

Any of your customers that are not on your standard list won't be missing much in the way of making you money by not being there, because they're already where you want them, in a prime position to buy a premium product from you. In my experience, customers are more than ten times more likely to buy from you again than your standard list, and this is the reason I said that your list is the least targeted and lowest quality of the big five resources.

3l. Customers To Long Term Customers

Moving on swiftly, lets look at the probably the most important part here, and that's turning your customers into long-term customers, or big buyers. Now just because they're in this phase and haven't bought your first high ticket item after standard follow-up procedures, doesn't mean they're useless, and will only ever buy the fifty dollar products from you. Far from it, but it does mean one of three things. Either there was a gap in your marketing system that they fell through, whether it was your intro product, your ad copy or your sales letter, or they couldn't afford to purchase the larger product, or finally they weren't interested in what you had to offer.

For those reasons, you have to make sure to cater to all of them when you launch your next products. They will receive your small intro product, and as a follow-up to this they will also receive your larger high-ticket product. This is important here, because if they didn't purchase your first high priced product, you'll want to get them in at the bottom again before you do anything else, and have them move through your intro product up to the bigger product. If your first time around was shoddy, they'll know your game, and not buy into the second fresh new product line you've set up, and never move through to buy high-ticket items from you.

Now as a follow-up to this, you'll want to also notify them directly about your high-ticket item some time after you notify them of the intro product. This way, you're again regenerating the trust and the familiarity of your brand through your intro product and at the same time, having those that didn't move up the ladder through your first product move up now. And of course don't go thinking that people will be annoyed that bought the intro product to receive a bigger, better product later, again for the reason that your intro product is a real, and helpful product, not just a cheap excuse to sell bigger stuff. It's ethical, it covers all angles relating to your standard customers, and what's more, it works like a charm.

3m. Turning Your Customers Into Joint Ventures.

Finally, turning your customers into joint venture prospects works in much the same way that you carried out for your list. You'll also be pulling research numbers from these guys, and from that research you'll know who to pull up for joint ventures. This is the only way to effectively do this and keep the joint ventures personal, instead of just mass mailing a list. It keeps you in the drivers seat. Of course, at this stage there's no other way to do this, chances are your list of customers who have purchased from you even though not as big as your list, will be too big to talk to all of them personally at this stage, which without this or affiliate stats, you have no other way of knowing who you want to make deals with.

3n. What To Do With Your Customers Summarized.

Summing this up then, your customers are important to you and have a specific role. Changing that role at this all important stage can do more harm than good. If you're going to contact them about anything other than research or sales of your products, refer to your research first and do it personally and individually for joint ventures, and avoid it altogether for turning them into affiliates. If you really want your customers to become affiliates as to plug the gap, make sure you have a higher commission integrated into the products they're buying from you, so they can take this offer up as a benefit if they're interested in the first place, and not to do it as afterthought.

Right, we're going to stop this one here as not to give you information overload. In the next section, after the summary that follows, we'll continue looking at how to cross your resources to get more out of them when we take a closer look at what to do (and what not to do) with your affiliates, long term customers and joint venture prospects. We'll also be taking a look at a few of the generalized ideas about treating all your lists correctly.

You'll see exactly what effect this has later, but I can tell you now, that when you launch into this type of cross promotion of your resources, you'll be drawing on all of this knowledge without having to wade through a bunch of text when you're busy launching your products and managing resources. It may seem a little strange right now, but I assure you, it's for the best, which you'll be finding out for yourself very soon. See you in the next section!

4. Exponential Resource Management 1. Summary.

• This whole section looks at cross promotion. Not as you may have been taught previously with other products, but this time, relating to the five resources you've been gathering.. What we're planning to do now is quickly and effectively bring your resources together in unison, and use the big five to multiply your promotion power many times over without having to ever bring any new resources in at all ultimately demonstrating how even if you have a small amount of resources, you can outperform someone with the same number and quality of resources by up to twenty five times.

• We're simply going to overlap each of them in a specific way so that each person becomes up to five times more profitable for you in five separate areas. What we'll also be doing at the end of the next section is providing you with an additional diagram that you can add to the previous one to give a more complete outlook of the whole resource movement and development process.

• Lets begin by immediately looking at the pro's and cons and the cross promotion of your list. Turning your list into affiliates,

customers, long term customers and joint
venture prospects.

• Your list. It's your first contact and your
base promotion power that contains everyone
that's ever passed through your site that hasn't
qualified for a specialty list (i.e. bought
something and landed themselves on the
customers list, or singed up as an affiliate and
landed on the affiliates list).

• They're all here, from freebie seekers, to
people that know what they've signed up for,
and those that don't, to those interested in
your business, to those interested in following
your progress and learning from you. It's
generally the most numerous of all the
resources and the lowest quality, but is an
essential starting point for filling the higher
ranks.

• Keep in mind that it's not always profitable
to expose one set of resources to another. This
is especially true for your most valuable
resources, for example, you wouldn't make a
strong effort to make your affiliates buy your
product, because that's not their role, and
you'll end up losing profitable affiliates for the
sake of a few thousands dollars of sales.

• So lets get started with your list now. What
do we want to turn your list into? Your list is

there for one thing and one thing only, to increase the other four main resources. Turning your list into customers and long term customers is straight forward, and all it requires is simple list maintenance and regular promotion. Quite obvious this one, but there's a few more things that you can do with your list that many don't utilize.

• The first. Build your affiliate base, and continue to build your joint venture base. Either of these that contain just one person that knows their stuff is more powerful than a list of ten or twenty thousand because of the power they have to make you (and themselves) profit compared to a lone ad of your own.

• This is why many successful and clued up business owners are willing to use at least half of their list announcements for building their other resources, simply because it's more profitable. The sooner you can begin to see that it's far easier to make a lot of money from building resources instead of making sales, and act on this information, the sooner you will begin to make the real money.

• My point here is especially with affiliate programs, if you have a high commission rate, (higher than the average 50-55% that is) and a worth talking about seventy percent plus, don't be afraid to tell your list about it.

• So whatever you do, don't think that gaining affiliates is all about that little button at the top of your sites with 80% for affiliates written in big letters. Hey, we spend money to promote free products to build our lists all the time, why can't we do the same for our affiliates? Well, we can, and we do for the reasons we outlined above.

• So the rule here is just this. If you're following the charts we've put up for you, this guide or a modified version of it, built around your own needs, and your commissions are higher than the average fifty percent, go ahead and make sure people know about it through your promotion. Even consider making it a prime concern of yours to get these affiliates instead of the profits through sales of your big product if you have the choice.

• Now moving on and as far as turning your list into joint ventures goes, this is also very powerful but also open ended and variable, because it's hard to know exactly what people are capable of when they're approaching you from your mailings.

• Try not to regulate your JV partners to those who visit your site and individuals picked through top performing affiliates, because there's a lot of potential elsewhere, namely in your other resources.

• For example, an experienced marketer that subscribes to a selection of lists to keep up with what's going on around them, happens to subscribe to your list where you're selling an info product such as this. He won't buy your small how to product, because he's got his system set up already and only promotes his own stuff to his list, unless it's a joint venture (this is very common among the big guys by the way), he won't buy your big product for the same reason, and he won't be joining your affiliate program for the above reason. He or she is a heavy hitter with a big list, but you're missing out. These are the people you're aiming to cater for here. It's not good if you're leaving massive holes like this, because you're missing out on some huge potential for profit.

• The problem with Jv's at this stage is it becomes kind of a lottery if you're not careful.

• You can't just send out a mailing asking for anyone with a list over ten thousand people to contact you for higher commissions, because then everyone else feels cheated and you may alienate some potential affiliates. In general terms joint ventures should be a private thing, the deal will also vary from person to person, depending on your product, their list size, what they want in return and what you can grant in return. The best way to go about this is to keep it that way. Don't do a mass mailing just requesting joint ventures for the reasons above, we can't do that for this particular resource.

• What I'd suggest you do instead, which you should be doing with your list anyway, is carry on as your normally do, sending out your un-intrusive surveys to help with your research and find out as much info as you can about the people on your list, for something in return.

For example a short valuable report that you've written on your area of expertise. In exchange you're getting vital info that not only allows you to tailor your ads to your list providing a better response rate, but at the same time you're building up a picture of who the good joint venture prospects are. Once you've done that, you can go through the results you've collected, and pick the top performers, the knowledgeable, and the people with the most resources, and contact them individually.

• As you can see your list is powerful, but not in the way most make out. Always remember your standard list is there to build your other resources, and isn't only for making straight up sales, which is where most seem to misplace the power of this tool.

• Lets move on now to the less obvious resources beginning with your customers. Immediately we know from prior knowledge that your customers have bought from you before, they're more trusting of you and your products and are in my personal experience over ten times more likely to buy from you again than the standard list.

• Be careful here, this is where we need to look hard at the role the customers play, because they're more valuable than your standard list in many ways, and often less numerous. For these reasons we have to get it right, because unsubscriptions are far more devastating here than for your standard list. You didn't spend all that time selling to them and building their trust just to scare them away again.

• So in the natural flow of things, where do your customers go next? Onto long term customers. As we discussed the added trust and stronger connection and involvement makes it far easier to sell higher priced items to standard customers. When they buy a second product from you, they turn into long term customers. They trust you, they spend often, and are likely to buy your products with the aim of profit in mind.

Often they'll stay with you for years buying again and again. It's immediately clear that the wrong move here can hurt your profits hugely, because is where most of it is coming from.

• So we already know the natural progression of things turns your customers into long term customers, but what about the other resources? Well for a start, I always find it handy to already have your customers on your standard list. You won't need to make much effort getting them there, because it's likely they'll have already subscribed to your stuff through your site, or the first product they purchased.

• This is useful though, because you can demonstrate to them through offers to customers only, that later reach the standard list that they're also on. I like to do this to emphasize my special offers for customers that have bought from me before are real, and the others don't get it, further increasing sales and enforcing trust. I would advise in addition to this to leave them on your standard list for this reason, as mailings to each resource should never be the same. Don't worry about making sure they're only on one list so you don't annoy them, they'll be happy to see they're special in this way of receiving offers in special mails that the standard list won't get.

• Next up, affiliates. Don't mistake your customers for affiliates. Understanding their role is so important here. A mailing here or there attached to your offer mentioning commissions is fine, but remember their role. They're here to buy your stuff and make you profit. More often than not they will either not know how to promote, or are more interested in buying than promotion. Keep this in mind, and always tailor your mailings to the role the customers play and concentrate on turning them into long-term customers. If you try too hard to direct their attention to affiliate programs and promotion, you're alienating the people who want to buy from you, and cutting off a main vein and one of the most important stages in actually making a profit at all.

• Finally, turning your customers into joint venture prospects works in much the same way that you carried out for your list. You'll also be pulling research numbers from these guys, and from that research you'll know who to pull up for joint ventures. This is the only way to effectively do this and keep the joint ventures personal, instead of just mass mailing a list. It keeps you in the drivers seat. Of course, at this stage there's no other way to do this, chances are your list of customers who have purchased from you even though not as big as your list, will be too big to talk to all of them personally at this stage, which without this or affiliate stats, you have no other way of knowing who you want to make deals with.

• In the next section we'll continue looking at these resources, and I'll show you how they begin to get even more powerful down the line compared to your list, often by hundreds of times.

• You'll see exactly what effect this has later, but I can tell you now, that when you launch into promotion, you'll be drawing on all of this knowledge without having to wade through a bunch of text when you're busy launching your products and managing resources. You'll be finding out for yourself very soon.

5. The Goals Of This Section

• To continue to look at and discuss effective ways of controlling, and using the resources that you're building through the launch of each product in such a way that you never have to worry about your promotion power ever again.

• To look at the reasons why many people can't get such a system in place, and why it hasn't been working for them, and what you're doing differently to ensure it does work.

• To further discuss the specific roles of each of your resources, allowing you more control over how you cross them over and have them build each other.

• To enhance the resource management sections and complete the picture of list, affiliate, customer, joint venture and long term customer management in such a way that's going to be highly beneficial to both your contacts, your business, and your pocket.

• To complete the sales system diagram by adding to it the flow of resources that will occur within your business when using this method.

- To sum up with a few pointers on how to treat each resource in general. Keep them happy, and how they'll keep you earning.

6. Exponential Resource Management 2.

In the last chapter, we looked at getting the most out of your five primary resources in such a way that they build themselves, but not just through other people promoting your stuff, but by the overlap of the resources through other means. We finished off talking about what to do with your standard customers, already having covered your list previously, so without further ado, we'll now continue further down the resources and talk about the remaining three and what you should or shouldn't be doing to make the most out of them. Please note, if you haven't read the previous section, you should do so, as this won't make any sense otherwise and you'll only get part of the picture.

6b. What To Do With Your Long Term Customers.

Ok next up along the line of resources comes your long term customers. At this point I'd usually tell you about how important long term customers are over something else, but as you may have noticed, they're all as important as each other, and you'll have a hard time keeping the numbers up effectively without a nice selection of each of the big five.

6c. Long Term Customers Into Affiliates

So, firstly, let's take a look at what you're going to do with your long term customers in regards to turning them into affiliates. Understand that when we talk about this, it may not be suitable to do so depending on your product. Turning any one of these resources into affiliates is especially important in the world of online marketing software or info selling, because after all, affiliate marketing is at least 20% of the whole picture. That's a huge chunk.

Well after telling you that I'm going to have to turn around now and tell you straight up that turning your long term customers into affiliates, (or trying to) is a bad idea. Remember, these people have already spent their money with you, and have seen your affiliate offers several times. Many of them will be on your list receiving the ads for your affiliate program solely, as we talked about earlier. For this reason there is absolutely no need to hassle these people directly with anything unnecessary.

Remember, this group has already spent a whole lot of money on your stuff, and if you want to keep them coming back, every time you contact them it has to be your best work. You need to be giving them something that they want, not just sending them ads ads ads. Also keep in mind, this particular list of yours should be the least numerous, but the biggest spenders.

Some of these people may come along to you and buy two thousand dollar product after two thousand dollar product. You can immediately see how valuable they are.

You can also see through a little math how much more devastating it is to annoy anyone on this list or cause them to leave for any reason. Granted, you may argue there's plenty more out there, but this is where most of your advertising funds are going. Getting people to buy your products that are going to be bringing you in a mighty profit in the first place isn't a short or easy task. Be very careful what you do with this list. This is going to be the long running theme in this section about your long term customers.

6d. Long Term Customers To Your List.

So how about turning long term customers into your list? Well, like I mentioned earlier, they are already on your list and most have generally followed the natural process of things, so there's no persuasion needed to that end. The problem comes when approaching them with your next products. What do you do? Remember in effect these people are a list in themselves, just think of them as your super high quality list as opposed to your standard, high numbers low return one.

Again, be very careful what you do with these people, and if you do mail them, make sure they first know they're valued and give them something for a free, also consider handing out discounts for future products, a reward scheme if you will, but remember to let them know why. Because they're valued. People like to feel valued, but if you don't tell them they are, then they're just going to assume you're another person, collecting more e-mail addresses, and sending them more ads.

6e. Long Term Customers Back Into Customers.

When it comes down to sending them ads when trying to sell them something else, things get a little more questionable. Do you start them in a system again, from the very beginning, or do you get them right in at the high priced end? That's exactly what I want to touch on right now. Turning your long term customers back into customers that first will purchase an entry level product, then be sold onto the full product. Do you, or don't you?

Well the answer is both a yes and no. I would suggest, for starters that you get them information out about your shiny new high ticket product. This is a great way to start getting some feedback before the masses start promoting and coming through the system onto this high priced product. Remember they've already spent their cash, and if your product was good, they already trust you and listen to you, and if your sales letter is good, you don't need to go through all that again, it serves no purpose.

The only time I would suggest that you start them from scratch all over again, is if it's been a long time since you've contacted them, or if you're going to be giving them something valuable for free therefore increasing the trust, and their feeling of special-ness further. For example, you've seen all those deals about people giving you bundles of stuff for free that's apparently supposed to be worth so much cash, so what's to stop you playing on that?

If you want to build trust with your long term

customers further, if your intro product plays too bigger part in your final high ticket product further down the chain than you can't afford to waive it, then give them your intro product. No, I'm not talking about something free that was free anyway, I'm talking take the $20-$60 out of your pocket that you're paying out in high commissions anyway from the intro product, and give it to them.

How often have you been given something for free by someone you bought something off of only to see them selling it later as a real product? How special would you feel as a valued customer to pick this up and watch another ad come through on a standard list the same day selling the brand new product you got free? Pretty special I'd imagine. I should say if you've succeeded in general in creating a form of bond with these people, then they'll start thinking you're worthwhile. It's not for us to decide who's worthwhile and who's not, it's the other way around. When this happens though, you'll find more people start talking to you, mailing you, calling you, and some pretty interesting stuff happens, in the form of...

6f. Long Term Customers To JV Prospects.

Turning your long term customers into joint venture partners, small or large, long term or short term. Keep in mind that this isn't by far your most effective way of generating joint ventures on a small scale, (ad swaps, list access etc) or even on a large scale (full blown partnerships of products, each playing a specialized role), however, you'd be surprised what happens when you start talking to people. This report for example wouldn't even be here if it wasn't for that factor alone.

Whilst we won't dwell on this for too long, I do want to make sure you understand I'm not telling you to go out, and start spending your day talking to your customers, and as anti professional as that sounds, we can't strike conversations up with all these people, especially as your business starts developing over a number of products, the numbers can get a little overwhelming if you're going to try and pull something like that out of your hat.

What I do want to make sure you understand though is to look for those signs that the long term customer that is contacting you would be a viable target for a joint venture offer, whether they mention they have a large list of their own, or on occasion you just get talking, and if it's with the right person, you might just find yourselves pulling some great ideas out of the bag together. Watch out for this, because it can, will and does happen more often than you may believe. I won't ramble on again at this stage about how important joint ventures are. Instead, lets move on to the next resource type in your arsenal.

6g. What to do with your affiliates.

Now we're getting to the interesting stuff. Affiliates are up next, and after running through the do's and don'ts of your paying customer base, things start to get a little more flexible here again, for simple reason that the situation is clear cut, and affiliates are more numerous than your long term customer base for example. By clear cut, I mean you know what these people want. They're here solely to promote a good product, and make good money doing so. You don't need to carry out any research to confirm that one.

Now, as far as turning your affiliates' attention to your list, I'm going to advise the same as previously just to make one hundred percent sure no one reading forgets that each of these resources should be a list in itself, with a clear goal, and a clear reason for being there. When you come to mailing them, you need to know what they want from you, as well as what you can give them in return. What we're not going to be doing in this particular case, is sending random adverts to your affiliates, not even for your products, because, as we learned earlier, they're more important than even your immediate profit, in fact, they're going to be the ones bringing in the majority of your new resources together with joint ventures (coming up next in the list).

We do however, get to send our affiliates ads of some sort, in fact very similar to the ads we talked about for your list, this time though, you're not trying to sell them on products to earn you hard cash, oh no, you're sending them ads to sell them on the promotion of you newest and latest products, not forgetting to mention to them how well your sales letter performs and giving them a nice visual picture of how much they can earn through your words. It might look different on the surface, but you're still selling them something, and all the rules you learn throughout this report apply to both monetary sales, selling free stuff, selling yourself and your products to gain joint ventures, or selling the potential to earn money through your affiliates. It's all about selling all the time.

That's enough covered to demonstrate my point, and we'll take it further in a moment when we go on to talk about joint ventures.

6h. Affiliates Into Customers.

Lets wrap up with the final three resources in the affiliates section, starting with customers. How on earth do you get your affiliates to pay you as well as promote for you? Well there's plenty of ways to turn these affiliates into customers. The first you would think would be looking at the intro product, and having affiliates that buy from you earn a higher commission. There's one problem with that though, what did we say the main goal of our intro product wasn't earlier on? if you remember we said that it's goal isn't to make a profit, but to build your resources.

Charging affiliates cash to join up, whether it be single sale, or membership using your intro product is cutting off your nose despite your face for this exact reason. This is especially true if you're attracting some heavy hitters and working in the online marketing info product world, not because they can't afford to buy your product, but because it's just a hassle compared to going in, filling in a quick form, promoting straight away. If you've been following us so far, and your affiliate commissions are nice and high to get lots of people promoting, you'll find that you won't be making much profit even if you did get them all to sign up. In any case, it's more likely you'll put them off promoting and lose some quick blasts to some of these peoples big lists if you go about this any other way. Steer clear of it, and remember the role of your intro products and the resource itself, your affiliates.

6i. Affiliates To Long Term Customers.

Looking at affiliates in the light of converting them to long term customers however, is a different story altogether, simply because that's what your long term product is there to do. Make you a profit, and if any of them sign up and buy this whilst promoting, while it'll be very unlikely it'll be the mainstay source of customers for your business, it can be a nice little bonus. How you do this is only limited by the system you have set up and your imagination, adaptation and implementation. There really is no right or wrong way, and to list every single method would be a whole encyclopedia in itself.

Let me give you some examples though so I don't leave you wonder what I'm talking about. First example, you want to make a profit out of your affiliates, so along with your next ad to them about the newest affiliate program you have released for your newest product goes an offer voucher for a discount, don't just want a boring old discount? Not a problem, how about the ticket only becomes valid when they've made five or ten sales.

Even better, instead of pushing affiliates hard, have the ticket only request one sale of your product before it becomes valid. It's very unlikely an affiliate with a good list is going to make exactly one sale when they blast an ad out. Easy they think, out goes the ad, ten sales come in instead of the one that they needed, they get a discount or even a free product on top of their commissions. At the same time, you persuaded someone to get out there and promote, not only bringing in more sales, but a bundle more resources that are going to do the same again and again. Best of all you were sleeping at the time. (I love that part)

Now ok granted you might be cringing at me right now wondering why I'm telling you this, but let me say in my defense, first think about what you're selling. If it's a Sixty dollar product, who cares if you give affiliates an 80% discount on top of their commission if they make a single sale. Remember that's not what we're talking about now. We're discussing high price items, anywhere from $500 to $10k per product. Now that discount starts to seem a little more significant and worthwhile. If I gave you 2k off one of my products on top of a 4k commission for making a single sale, would you blast an ad to your private, targeted list about that? There's a whopping wad of cash in it for you, and potentially hundreds more people for me to sell my products to for me.

It doesn't even have to go that far, even if you're only selling a $1250 product. When was the last time you were paid $500 per sale you made? If you have been paid that much before, I bet the product you were selling was pretty successful. Why don't more people pull stuff like this off? Simply wait until you've sold as many as you can in a short period of time, then open it up for affiliates with a deal like this while the buzz is still there about your product.

6j. Affiliates Into JV's.

Finally in the affiliates resource crossing list, lets look at our final resource with a view to turn affiliates into a joint venture partners.

This is real easy to do, and it's quick and painless for you. All it involves is either a simple phone call, or personal e-mail. Now we're getting into rare, doesn't happen every day, gotta make this meeting as personal as possible territory.

What you're looking out for is a high rate of sales through your affiliate software. A simple search should do that if you've chosen a good system. Pick out the top two percent that have really made a dent and will generally make up the numbers big time and keep them handy. Not only should you have already rewarded them, but you should keep them ready and waiting for your next product, especially if it's related to your previous one.

If they did a good job promoting your previous product, it generally means they have the resources and ability to continue. You should be there when they decide that with a pre-empted contact prior to the release of your shiny new product, offering first stab at promotion and higher commissions than the norm. You may even be able to figure something else out if they have something you want. I can't detail that here, every joint venture is different. Make of it what you need of it. The deal doesn't all have to be higher commissions and more money more money all the time.

If you could have anything right now that would move you towards your goals more quickly, or in an easier way, what is it? Does this person I'm dealing with have it? If the answer is no, a safe bet is always the standard higher commissions. And remember, why are you giving them a load of special-ness, over standard affiliates? Because they're valued affiliates. They probably know it already, but it doesn't half hit home when you say it, especially, as in the above example in the customers resource crossing section, when they see the standard offer going out to all the other affiliates (they will be on the same list still after all). That'll sure show them that you're for real, they won't forget you either. Treat them right and they'll continue to make you a whole load of money for many years to come, and provide some really fruitful joint venture proposals and deals.

6k. What To Do With Your JV Prospects.

Talking of joint venture deals, lets move on now to the fifth and final section on crossing your resources over and talk about the do's and do not's of probably the most lucrative marketing method in the business. Of the big five, your joint venture prospects and partners will likely be the least numerous of all your resources, but with the most stopping power per person. When you think that some of your JV's might end up being seen by lists of ten to a hundred thousand or more, it suddenly becomes clear how important this is. Lets look at where to take your joint ventures with regards to the other four resources, starting with affiliates.

6l. Turning Your JV's Into Affiliates.

First up, you should keep in mind that most joint ventures that you receive after launching your fist two products will come from your affiliates anyway. As far as those who don't, they're really glorified affiliates only. As with the difference between customers and long term customers, you'll find that even with those who aren't your affiliates, you'll be in contact with them pretty frequently anyway, whether they're on your instant messenger list, or you just fire emails at each other when you each launch new products.

Building up a circle of contacts that act in this way is extremely powerful in itself, just it takes a little more time to set up when it comes to product launches. Maintenance won't be a problem if you're using good affiliate software, so in this respect, keep your joint venture prospects separate. They're something special, and you'll likely find yourself in contact with them even more so than your long term customers, and they will be your first line of attack when launching future products. So when it comes to turning JV's into regular affiliates, don't bother, because they're all that and more already.

6m. Turning Your JV's Into Your List.

Secondly, turning joint ventures into your list. Not something to dwell on, because your joint ventures shouldn't be a list themselves. They should be a selection of business people that have access to resources that are beneficial to your business, not a bunch of e-mail addresses that you fire out ads to. Some may be on your list already, those that like to see what you're getting up to and when, and some may not. Either way, it doesn't matter, and you should never be thinking of your joint ventures as just a list of e-mail addresses. Things should be far more personal than that, at a cost of set up time to you, but producing some major profits and massive resource building potential.

6n. Not Turning Your JV's Into Customers.

Moving straight on to the section I've been itching to tell you about, and that's moving joint ventures over to become your customers and long term customers. It's possible that some may have bought from you before, or even learned how to promote from you if your products are geared towards that way of thinking, however, your joint venture partners are way too important to go advertising to unless it's in a 'hey check it out, thought you might find it interesting' kind of way.

Let me tell you a little story about how not to do this. I used to work with a few people when I first started, and we were getting along fine, we created a few sites, experimented and compared notes a lot, and things were going great until I decided to branch out on my own. At regular intervals over the next three or four months whilst I was working on building my affiliate software, I started to receive interesting e-mails and messages from these people. Now understand that we were business colleagues, kind of like the people you talk to and hang around with and take your lunches with and had a laugh with at work.

Unfortunately that all changed pretty quickly, and although I was still getting the personal one on one deals from these people, they were trying to hard sell me. You can imagine logging on to the net and receiving mails or Instant Messages from one of your old friends that contained sales letter patter and hard sell messages. This is not how joint ventures are supposed to be carried out. It's inevitable, once you've been in contact with people for a period of time, you find yourself more relaxed and chatting more like friends, even though you both know business is the underlying subject.

So here's the deal, no matter how short of cash you get, no matter how much you think they're going to spend, don't hard sell or give your joint ventures sales pitches. Remember what they're there for. Mutual deals that benefit both your products and businesses. Remember, this doesn't necessarily mean you can't tell them about your new stuff or a new product someone has released, but watch the way you go about it.

It's immediately obvious once you've been around a while when someone you know is trying to sell something to you in this manner. Sure, contact me, tell me about your new stuff, and show me the new opp you joined, tell me how it's going and what the word is on the net, ask me if I'm interested in joining you, not a problem, but the moment you start talking to me about how much of a stunningly amazing deal I'm getting, and how it's going to EXPLODE my sales by 400% overnight, guaranteed! Expect me to raise an eyebrow at you, turn around, and walk away. Moral of the story, watch what you're saying and how you're saying it if you want to keep your joint venture partners close.

60. The Final Diagrams.

Alright, do you now see how each resource can go on to become relevant in two sections, double the promotion power for you, but at the same time you have to be very careful not to go over the top, or make a wrong move when trying to cross your resources over. Some of the above are obvious, and will lose you your resources in a particular way, and some of the less obvious have time based constraints which as pointed out in the relevant sections, and will have you messing with confusing tangled balls of resources that aren't viable compared to the amount of profit they bring you. Before moving on to three general rules about treating your customers correctly, here's the chart to demonstrate in note form what we've just talked about above and the previous chapter for each of your resources.

Note: This is not some fancy marketing system that's been created for the sake of doing so. It simply demonstrates one of the fundamentals of every manual I've ever written. Your resources, and how when they're building each other, you can never say you have no one to promote to, no one to promote your stuff, no one to strike deals with, and no way to make profit, because you do have all of those things. It's all here, ready and waiting.

6p. Three Treating Your Customers Right Concepts.

Ok, finally before moving on to the next subject, and wrapping up this section, I'd like to talk to you about three, very general concepts relating to how to and how not to treat your customers, with a view to getting the most out of each every one of them through your marketing. I'd like to start off by giving you a quick run down of freebie syndrome and giving away the world.

Freebie syndrome as I call it, unfortunately seems to be almost incurable over short periods of time. This occurs when you give too much for to little to your resources. Generally, the people that do this are in the mindset that people will remember them, thank them and like them for giving things to them. It's important however that no matter what resource you're dealing with not to do this too regularly for starters, and secondly don't give away anything worth more than around sixty dollars at the absolute max, especially when the product is new.

If you find yourself starting to do this, whether it's with affiliate commissions, mailings to your list, or being too kind to your customers or even your joint venture prospects and contacts, you'll likely see that they start to take it for granted and come to expect it, only to suddenly be offended when you don't keep up the pattern. Remember this if you're giving freebies away, make sure people know that it's a special thing that you don't do very often. This not only adds even more value to your words and products, but inoculates against freebie syndrome from the start, and you won't have to keep giving away the world to keep everyone happy.

Lastly, and quite simply, keep in touch. I'm not suggesting you mail your resources every day, or even every week, but I'd suggest keeping in contact at least three or four times a month minimum without making that fatal mistake of sending out e-mails when you have nothing to say. If you don't do this, gradually, over time, people will forget that trust you've built up with them, or even worse, forget who you are altogether, or not remember to update their accounts and subscriptions with their new contact details.

6q. Wrapping Up.

Generally they're more likely to remember you the further down the resource chart they are, and the more you should be doing to make sure they stay this way. That about wraps it up for how to treat your customers. I hope you'll agree that we've just talked through something far more important than customer service techniques here. We've just covered how to get your resources to build each other internally. Couple this with the external building and the influx of new customers you're receiving through your new products, and you'll find yourself in an abundance of promotion power.

7. Section Summary.

• Greetings, and welcome to treating your customers right part two, where we'll be looking at the final three resource types, and how to cross them over in the most profitable way, multiplying their profitability by five and potentially, massively multiplying your profits at the same time.

• Let's jump in immediately, and having already talked about the list and your short term customers, lets discuss your long term customers and the relationship they have with your other four resources.

• The first thing I want to talk about is trying to turn your long term customers into heavy hitting affiliates. The best thing to do here is avoid trying to do that.

• For the reasoning behind this, we first need to refer back to the role that long term customers play in your business. Couple your long term customers and place them in the same category as your standard customers. They're special, your money makers, the people who are purchasing your products.

• For this reason we need to treat them as such. Trying to get the most affiliates as quickly as possible may seem like a good idea in the beginning, but when we take a closer look, we know that such actions can go towards removing the role of your customers especially, and when we do things that count towards unsubscriptions especially when looking at your profit pullers, this is not a good move.

• If anything, leave them be, use them to promote your products and place the commission levels on a big red button on your site, as we discussed previously avoiding any unnecessary unsubscriptions through wrongly crossing your resources.

• You can also see through a little math how much more devastating it is to annoy anyone on this or cause them to leave for any reason. Granted, you may argue there's plenty more out there, but this is where most of your advertising funds are going. Getting people to buy your products that are going to be bringing you in a mighty profit in the first place isn't a short or easy task. Be very careful what you do with this list. This is going to be the long running theme in this section about your long term customers.

• So how about turning long term customers into your list? Well, treating long term customers is very similar to the way in which you're treating your first time customers, because they're so closely related and generally have the same role; to make you profit through the products they buy now and into the future, the reaction here is the same.

• Don't worry about trying to separate them, instead use the fact that most will be on your standard list through your other subscription methods to your advantage to build trust, and prove your special previous customers only offers really do mean previous customers only. Straight forward enough, but there is a difference here, and something that I'd like to talk about is what do you do with them after they've bought their second product.

• Do you start them at an intro product and work them up again? Or do you sell them straight onto the follow-up profit making products? In effect, do you turn your long term customers back into customers through less expensive products, or turn your long term customers back into long term customers straight up?

• Well the answer is mixed. It's both to be exact. The general consensus on the matter is they should indeed receive immediate notification on the launch of your follow-up products. After all, they already have the trust factor three, so there's no reason that they shouldn't buy these high priced products from you. There's no need to demote them to standard customers again.

• There is only one situation in which it's best to start them all over again, and that's if you haven't contacted them for a long time. This should be taken care of in your list maintenance however, as you should be in touch with your list, customers and long term customers at the very least once every two weeks to prevent the evaporation of this trust that you've worked hard to build.

• There is another way to build trust further with your long term customers, and that's to give them something free. Now I'm not talking the standard freebie with a made up price on it, but in fact your intro product that you're selling for sixty dollars or so to your standard customers. This is especially helpful as a booster after the initial ad for a high ticket item, because it allows you to convert extra sales through the intro product. You have nothing to gain any longer by actually selling these products to your long term customers, but everything to gain when you consider giving them your intro product further inspires trust when they see it come down for the other list members at a cost, and secondly, by converting those extra sales when your intro product is tailored to selling onto the higher priced product. Sales coming from every angle, just what we like to see.

- Next, lets move on and talk about turning your long term customers into one of the most powerful resources you can have at your disposal. Joint venture prospects. Many would disagree with me when I say long term customers are a good source of joint venture prospects, but through my personal experience, I have to disagree.

- Now there isn't much that you actively have to do here aside from passively watch out for the signs. It isn't unlikely that you may have contact with some of your long term customers, more so than any of the resources we've discussed so far.

- Even though this isn't the quickest or most effective way of pulling Jv's from your resources, it's still quite possible. There's nothing much that I can say aside from you'd be surprised what happens when you begin talking to people, especially your long term customers, some of which I've now been in personal contact with since my first site back in '99/2000.

- So don't go out there looking, but look out for signs such as mentions of having large amounts of promotion resources themselves, or mentions of their previous experiences, or even if you just happen to get talking, which has happened to me on a number of occasions, more often than you might expect.

• Lets move on to the next resource type and one of the most interesting and pliable of the lot. Your affiliates.

• This is where things begin to get interesting and flexible too. The reason being when looking out for affiliates and converting affiliates into different resources you have a lot more to work with as far as the numbers are concerned and it's much easier to pick out and approach them yourself safe in the knowledge you're approaching the best performers. It's clear cut. They signed up with you to promote your products and make themselves a bundle of cash, making you a bundle of cash at the same time.

• Beginning with the least effective, and that's turning your affiliates into your list. As far as affiliates go, they're the least likely to be on your list as well as on your affiliates list compared to the other resources, because a majority of them are there for the promotion opportunity instead of the products themselves unlike your customers, long term customers and standard list. The only time that this may not be true is when you're in online marketing to teach online marketing. Many of your students and purchasers may become your affiliates too.

• What we're not going to be doing in this particular case, is sending random adverts to your affiliates, not even for your products, because, as we learned earlier, they're more important than even your immediate profit, in fact, they're going to be the ones bringing in the majority of your new resources together with joint ventures.

• Remembering that each of these resources is a list of their own anyway, you will be sending out communications, jump starts and offers to get and keep affiliates promoting.

• Before getting to the good parts lets take a look at turning your affiliates into customers and long term customers.

• If you've been following us so far, and your affiliate commissions are nice and high to get lots of people promoting, you'll find that you won't be making much profit even if you did get them all to sign up. In any case, it's more likely you'll put them off promoting and lose some quick blasts to some of these peoples big lists if you go about this any other way. Steer clear of it, and remember the role of your cheap introductory and purely resource building products, and the resource itself, your affiliates.

• Looking at affiliates in the light of converting them to long term customers however, is a different story altogether, simply because that's what your high priced product is there to do. Make you a profit, and if any of them sign up and buy this whilst promoting, while it'll be very unlikely it'll be the main source of customers for your business, it can be a nice little bonus. How you do this is only limited by the system you have set up and your imagination, adaptation and implementation. There really is no right or wrong way, and to list every single method would be a whole encyclopedia in itself.

• An example of this would be a discount or even a free product after making a number of sales. Remember not to substitute this for their commissions or any other special offers at any point, because it's extremely unlikely that this will be a large source of income anyway, and you have to be careful not to take away the number one reason they're your affiliates, and that's to make money for their pocket.

• A good method to adopt is instead of pushing affiliates hard, is to have the ticket only request one sale of your product before it becomes valid. It's very unlikely an affiliate with a good list is going to make exactly one sale when they blast an ad out. Easy they think, out goes the ad, ten sales come in instead of the one that they needed, they get a discount, you persuaded someone to get out there and promote, not only bringing in more sales, but a bundle more resources that are going to do the same again and again.

• Finally in the affiliates section lets look at turning your affiliates into joint ventures. A very powerful technique indeed, looking back to what we approached earlier in this section when talking about the ease of this method due to your knowledge of their performance simply through their sales.

• A really simple way to comb your affiliates for good JV prospects is after a number of weeks of promotion, check your affiliate stats, select the top ten and approach them. Tell them that they're in the top ten, and that your next product has just been released, and you want them to promote. Because of their past performance you have already raised the commissions on their account by ten or fifteen percent compared to the regular promotions.

• This is also a very viable tactic after a few weeks of promotion for the same product, but remember to take your affiliates with you no matter what you launch, because wherever they go is where your ads will reach the most people, and also where your ads will pull in the most resources for future promotion further building your arsenal without pulling money out of your pocket for paid ads. See how easy this is once you've got started, and how important it is to understand already? Where others are spending all their time and money getting started again and again, you're here letting your resources build themselves. You may be giving away higher commissions but you're getting equals back in return through the gain in promotion power.

• Remember also that just because your affiliates are not turning into other resources directly, they are indirectly building your resources through their promotions. This is the main importance of affiliates aside from making direct sales, and what makes them so powerful in building your resources for you compared to the standard list or your customers and long term customers.

• Ok lets move on to the final resource, and that's your Jv's, comprised of all sorts of marketers that have come from every other resource, top affiliates especially. Some of which you approached, and some approached you, their promotion power is as immense as the affiliate, but on an even higher level. The least numerous and most personal of your resources. When you think that some of your JV's might end up being seen by lists of ten to a hundred thousand or more, it suddenly becomes clear how important this is.

• First and foremost, we don't turn our Jv's into our list full stop. Again, through their promotion they may build your list as a resource, and they may jump on it if they want to keep an eye on your progress and your business, but aside from that, we're never bulk mailing these people, even when making deals, because each one is tailored to each individual product and you and your JV prospect. It's simply different every time, and heck, most of these people won't need to be on your JV list anyway because they're going to end up working with you and communicating with you through more personal and direct means.

• Next turning your Jv's into affiliates is moot, because generally they are an extended form of affiliates; promotion for specific deals instead of the standard commissions. Due to their promotion power they always get something extra, so shouldn't be grouped in with your affiliates at any stage.

• Ok here comes the good bit, my fave part of the whole lot that I've been itching to tell you about. Turning your JV's into customers and long term customers. The number one thing that I can think of that in my experience many attempt, but attempt totally one hundred percent incorrectly.

• It's possible that some may have bought from you before, or even learned how to promote from you if your products are geared towards that way of thinking, however, your joint venture partners are way too important to go advertising to unless it's in a 'hey check it out, thought you might find it interesting' manner.

• Here's a little something that might get you thinking. Imagine you've been working with five people for a year or two on your businesses, JV'ing with them and such. Then one day, along comes four of them, up pops a message on your IM program. They do the standard meet and greet, and then comes the moment you've been waiting for. Along comes the hard sell. A corny cliché passage from a sales letter, and a very obvious scripted sales process. Bear in mind these are the people you've worked with and talked to as if they were friends in a business sense for long periods of time and have already built a good business relationship with them.

• What would your reaction be if your wife or

your husband, or even one of your friends tried to hard sell you on something with typical sales patter? It's not very nice I can tell you that. I should warn you at this stage too, if you go on to take this information and be a success, some of the people you've been working with and have been friendly with for some time might even adopt a hard sell approach with you, when on a normal day they would have just said 'Hey, check out my new product' in a friendly manner. 'Are you up for a deal, maybe an ad to your list if I whack your commissions above the norm?'. Or even, 'hey some guy sent me an ad for this yesterday <insert link here> I thought it looked cool, check it out if you have time'.

• That's all it takes. A quick, straight up, not beating around the bush or wasting time, non hard sell like mention or offer. The moment you try to hard sell a JV, they stop being your JV partners and contacts and you demote them to standard list members. When you begin to launch your own products and this happens to you, you'll spot it a mile off.

• It's immediately obvious once you've been around a while when someone you know is trying to sell something to you in this manner. Sure, contact me, tell me about your new stuff, and show me the new op you joined, tell me how it's going and what the word is on the net.

Ask me if I'm interested in joining you, not a problem, but the moment you start talking to me about how much of a stunningly amazing deal I'm getting, and how it's going to EXPLODE my sales by 400% overnight, guaranteed! expect me to raise an eyebrow at you, turn around, and walk away. Moral of the story, watch what you're saying and how you're saying it if you want to keep your joint venture partners close, and your current marketing contacts would be wise to do the same for you to avoid negative effect. If you begin to get hard sells from your contacts, don't fret, just relax and walk away. If they're hard selling their close contacts it's likely they don't know what they're doing anyway and it isn't worth your time to worry about.

• Much like affiliates, as you can see the higher we get up the resource chain, the more important the resource becomes, and the less you can actually turn your affiliates and Jv's into, but the more of your resources they build for you through deals and promotion anyway.

• We've just covered how to get your resources to build each other internally. Couple this with the external building and the influx of new customers you're receiving through your new products, while others are struggling to start again, spending loads of cash and time trying to get started each time they launch a new product, and you'll find yourself with an abundance of promotion power, now and far into the future.

www.ingramcontent.com/pod-product-compliance
Lightning Source LLC
Chambersburg PA
CBHW071229220526
45468CB00002B/786